Orient Point

Also by Julie Sheehan

Thaw

To Meredith,
Fellow traveller toward

that ever elusive

Orient Point !

Julie Sheehan

Hofstra Un.

July 2008

W. W. NORTON & COMPANY

NEW YORK   LONDON

For information about permission to reproduce selections from this book,
write to Permissions, W. W. Norton & Company, Inc.,
500 Fifth Avenue, New York, NY 10110

Manufacturing by Courier Westford
Book design by Lovedog Studio
Production manager: Anna Oler

Library of Congress Cataloging-in-Publication Data

Sheehan, Julie.
Orient point / Julie Sheehan.— 1st ed.
p. cm.
Poems.
ISBN-13: 978-0-393-06191-8 (hardcover)
ISBN-10: 0-393-06191-4 (hardcover)
I. Title.
PS3619.H44O75 2006
811'.6—dc22

2006001416

W. W. Norton & Company, Inc.
500 Fifth Avenue, New York, N.Y. 10110
www.wwnorton.com

W. W. Norton & Company Ltd.
Castle House, 75/76 Wells Street, London W1T 3QT

1 2 3 4 5 6 7 8 9 0

Mother??? Dad?? They're in the wings blowing kisses at me. Holding up signs. "You've never played better."

—*John Guare*

Contents

II. ARCHEOLOGY

III. FINE PRINT

Acknowledgments

Barrow Street (winter 2002): "Correspondence"

Briar Cliff Review (vol. 15, 2003): "Mary at the Well"

Commonweal (Dec. 20, 2002): "Maurice Greene, The Fastest Man Alive, Is Asked the Secret of His Success," "Harriet Tubman"

The Journal (fall/winter, 2005): "It Was a Normal Day Except I Fell"

Kenyon Review (summer 2005): "Loose Leaf from a Destroyed Journal"

Literary Imagination (winter 2005): "Honeymoon in the Grenadines"

Mississippi Review (spring 2004): "Coney Island, VI: Fine Print at the Bottom of the Contract"

Nebraska Review (vol. 33:1, 2005) "Ivory-Billed Woodpecker," "Sonnet: To a Young Refugee, Upon Finding Asylum in the Midwest," "Rural Development News"

Paris Review (fall 2003): "Brown-Headed Cowbirds" (winner, Bernard F. Conners Prize for Poetry)

Parnassus (vol. 28, nos. 1&2, 2005): "St. Philomena"

Pleiades (vol. 24: no. 2, 2004): "Hate Poem"

Raritan (winter 2005): "Polar Bear in the Central Park Zoo," "Coyotes in Greenwich!"

Rattapallax (no. 8, Sept. 2002): "Candling Eggs," "Details of Cana"

Salmagundi (spring–summer 2005): "Sonnet: To a Marriage That Cannot Be Saved by a Weekend in Calistoga"

Southwest Review (vol. 90, no. 1, 2005): "Mercy School"

Yale Review (July 2003): "Archaic Smile"

"Hate Poem" reprinted in *180 More: Extraordinary Poems for Every Day*, ed. with an introduction by Billy Collins. Random House, New York: 2005. Also reprinted in *The Best American Poetry 2005*, series ed. David Lehman, guest ed. Paul Muldoon. Scribner, New York, NY, 2005.

"Stray" published in *We Thank You, God, for These: Prayers and Blessings for Family Pets, An Anthology*. Paulist Press, New York: 2003.

I would like to thank all of the generous souls who have helped this manuscript along its way, especially Gaby Calvocoressi, Scott Hightower, Richard Matthews, Debbie Nelson, and Robert Thomas, for their tough love in reading early versions of the poems; a battery of teachers, mentors, and editors, including Neil Azevedo, Angela Ball, Jill Bialosky, Harold Bloom, Bob Boyers, Lucie Brock-Broido, Patricia Carlin and the *Barrow Street* gang,

George Howe Colt, Alfred Corn, Rosemary Deen, Jeanne Emmons, Kathy Fagan, Linda Gregg, John Hollander, Bob Holman, Mike Janeway, Joy Katz, Jackson Lears, Herb Leibowitz, Richard Locke, David Lynn & David Baker, J. D. McClatchy, Martin Mitchell, Kevin Prufer, Alice Quinn, Sarah Spence, and Willard Spiegelman, for guidance and inspiration they may not realize they had supplied; Sharon Olds and the Poetry Society of America for support through the Robert H. Winner Memorial Award; Bokara Legendre and the Medway Institute for their support; Richard Howard and Marie Ponsot, who have been teacher, mentor, and editor all at once; a stalwart network of friends, without whose sanity mine would have been imperiled, including the College Chums, Michael Dorsey, Susan Gruber, Alison Ingram, Ellen Korbonski, Julie Raynor, Joyce Shulman & Eric Cohen, Andrew Solomon and my family, including Robert and Sarah, Rev. John Sheehan, my son Miles, and my mother and father, Rosemary and Jim Sheehan, to whom this book is dedicated.

I

Taxidermy

Honeymoon in the Grenadines

At last we round the point, the outboard choking
under the free hand on its throttle, hull slapping along,
our guide's face incongruously merry over the clatter.

We know what we will see before we see it,
a cove's great gleam, the crescent of beach, common
as flour, almost guaranteed in these parts, like this boat,

almost guaranteed, no shabbier than the next, and painted
such a clamorous shade of blue we had to choose it.
So here we are, bouncing toward the expected

fine white powder. Nearing, our boatman cuts the motor,
which dies the comedic death of a popgun, gratefully.
Now we bob shoreward, closer, the sand clarifying

to a pebbly grain, like those white bedspreads
everyone used to have. Still closer, the empty beach
looks positively crowded, bumped, knobby, difficult,

not sand's posh shunting-off of shape, but heaped—
with chalk, perhaps? rocks? odd round bones?
No, conch shells—I see now—compose that beach;

big ones, too, giftshop-sized, the tourists would love them.
How did they get here, these bleached and hardened
corpses, these beached white miniature whales?

Why, there are piles of them, sharp as martyrs, I'd think,
and look! A man walking on them! We look.
Our guide looks, too, his cheer undiminished:

everything's normal. He does not see what we see,
the excess to which these conch shells are unwanted,
the drifts of them, the waste—beautiful objects

yanked from reef, slitted to slide out those ugly
slugs, discarded by the thousands, the millions,
to fill a few slop pails with their velvet viscera.

Look at you, husband, in your linen and straw,
and me, with insides only another culture could love.
I'm chilly now, let's go back. Our guide protests,

his fat fee evaporating in the happy sun,
but already someone else is taking our place.
Nor does he care to know what it is we flee:

the long white warp, the one man black against it
who jerks a shell over his shoulder, bends to evict another,
heeds not their whispered roar: *our hearts are empty.*

Maurice Greene, the Fastest Man Alive, Is Asked the Secret of His Success

He answers almost before the question's out,
neither jumping the gun, nor waiting around
　　for the undulation of sound

to lap him, but, surging on the still moment
of the thought's articulation, he foots
　　the border of start and stop.

This urge to meet the upward lilts of questions,
to train them with trochaic ankle weights,
　　this deliberative slash

toward finishing things is over in a flash:
　　Patience, he says. Patience is at last
what it takes to win the hundred-yard dash.

Brown-Headed Cowbirds

(As Identified by *The Audubon Society Field Guide
to North American Birds*)

> *This species and the Bronzed Cowbird are the only
> North American songbirds that are brood parasites,
> laying their eggs in the nests of other birds and leaving
> them to the care of foster parents.*

Out of the imagination,
Out of the brooding brain,
Out of the urban nest, lined in desires scaveng'd
    from American soil, woven
    in thorniest tree,
Out of instinct springen strange birds, strange birds
    though common, foster birds,
    siren birds, their songs ruinous,
Out of neglect and knowledge of neglect, and the outward
    show of caring
They comen, seeking survival.

> *Unlike parasitic Old World cuckoos, which lay eggs
> closely resembling those of a host species, cowbirds lay
> eggs in the nests of over 200 other species, most smaller
> than themselves.*

Bifel that enrollen them in the Anti-Violence Program,
    pursuing Romance,

Three tough girls of twelve, invited forthwith to enroll,
Three lumpish girls most terrifying of hallway,
   fastest to grow, and dangerously large, and ythrust
     into fifth grade with the smaller ones;
Three screeching with arrogance unearned, valor unloved.

Ful gladly enrollen they in the Anti-Violence Program,
   for it containeth a Theater Component
   as mandated by the Most Rightful
   and Honorable Board of Ed;
For the sacred Subparagraphs have made it so.

And each girl dreameth of Whitney Houston and Jennifer Lopez,
That she may one day flouteth the midriff of Brittany Spears;
They liken themselven as to the goddesses;
They storm the Pantheon as unto a sparrow's nest;
They practice afore mirrors, bejewel themselven with hope,
Bejewel their dusky bellies, someday sanctuaries
   of the handball boys
  who will nest their sweaty heads thereupon,
  who will see at last the ful queenliness
   of the brown-headed cowbird,
  who will offer gold earrings and fall down
   in adoration.

And the girls are yclept Shaquina, Latisha, Quanesha,
And the first name deriveth from "Sha" and "Nika,"
   syllables magnificent in sound

although without sense;
And the second name issueth forth from the union
of "La" and "Tisha," syllables also magnificent,
which additionally lighten upon
the Latin word for joy;
And the third, Quanesha, ariseth from the American
"Qu" plus "Aisha," both meanings unknown,
although beauteous indeed.

And the threesome writeth their names upon the sign-up sheet;
They embellish their "i"s with hearts (except Quanesha,
who draweth a flower inside her "Q," for she hath
no "i");
They anticipate the starring role, Juliet the doomed one,
Juliet the goddess;
They will all play Juliet to the handball boys' Romeos.

And at the first meeting they are cast as Capulets
who speaken most hotly, most warlike
to Montagues;
For the Theater Component hath an Anti-Violence motif;
all of the love scenes are cut.

Some host species eject the unwanted egg, others lay down a new nest lining over it, but most rear the young cowbird as one of their own.

And the girls attempt to quit, but it is too late; they are adopted;
    the assistant principal hath recorded their names,
    the visiting theater artist hath received her stipend,
    the handball boys have committed infractions
        withalle, and languish in detention.

Bifel that rehearsen the girls; on occasion they rehearse;
    between trips to the bodega, they rehearse:
        to wit the biting of thumbs at one another;
        to wit the barbs verbal, talon'd as fingers;
        to wit the unquenched fire of pernicious rage,
            purple like martins;
They ronnen through scenes familiar from the neighborhood,
    the fisticuffs and scramble,
    the outgrown bicycles barreling down upon trikes,
    the pigtails ytrounced by plump cornrows,
    the Double Dutch push, the Double Dutch shove.

And everichoon knoweth in her heart, *I am the best actress!*
In the certainty of twelve years of life she knoweth ful wel;
Bifel that Shaquina, Latisha and Quanesha each proclaimeth
    I am the best actress!
And yieldeth not, and speaketh most hotly and warlike
    of the next one's faults,
And taunteth each the others, and swinge them soundly.

And the visiting theater artist rusheth to soothe, to placate, to becalm,
She raineth Positive Feedback upon their rage that it may be
    ysquelched.
(They remember not her name, this visitor from other worlds
    who flieth in and flieth out, her beak stuffed with morsels,
They her clepen *Miss*;
Even so, her fondness for them prevaileth.)
And gabblen the girls their cheeky *check,* and prattle they
    Miss, Miss,
    I am the best actress, right Miss?
And Miss replieth not, for fear her students flee
    to the bodega,
    and shirken the rehearsal.

> *The young cowbird grows quickly at the expense of the
> young of the host, taking most of the food or pushing
> them out of the nest.*

Time passeth, bifel that the girls voyage to the City-Wide
    Anti-Violence Summit Conference;
And they are unprepared, yet goen forth they cocksure of greatness;
And the Capulets and Montagues of P.S. 175 flock unto
    the Capulets and Montagues of P.S. 51 and P.S. 126;
And each girl who knoweth her virtues in her heart
    proclaimeth to all:
    I am the best actress!
Shaquina, Latisha and Quanesha proclaimen ful loudly:
    I am the best actress!

But Kaisha, Jolanda and Deshawna, three others, are also
    each the best actress,
The Summit Conference teemeth with best actresses;
And Kaisha, Jolanda and Deshawna speak hotly: *Get thee
    gone,* they avouch, *for thy acting is shite!*
Aroint thee, witch! responden Shaquina, Latisha
    and Quanesha, *for I am the best actress!*

And the Capulets and Montagues of various schools clear out,
    and maken a rough circle,
And the best actresses squabble in their midst,
    the best actresses and most valorous;
And the Anti-Violence Summit Conference will invite
    P.S. 175 no more.

> *It has been suggested that cowbirds became parasitic
> because they followed roving herds of bison and had no
> time to stop to nest.*

Look to thy purse, mend thy ways, O Board of Ed:
Though thou hast spent lavishly, yet hast thou failed to consider
    the roving herds of bison;
    the facts of survival; the persuasion of habitat;

Look to thy bond and sin no more, visiting theater artist:
    thou hast starved thine own young;

Look to thyselven, Shaquina, Latisha, thy brown heads
    tall among the blond, the blood drying brown

on thy feet where thou tramplest,
stalking victorious in thy feather'd cage;
Look to thy virtue, Quanesha, for the handball boys
comen, fleet
and hard and adoring, with gold in their talons
and no time to nest.

Sonnet: To a Young Refugee, Upon Finding Asylum in the Midwest

By now he's mastered open space. He hunches
in Michigan's fair-haired classroom taking notes,
a windbreaker hung among the overcoats,
a concentration, solo at his lunch.

He chews alone, he swallows alone, pristine
he talks to no one. When they call out sides
for dodgeball he dissolves, lets his spirit glide
like a fine sword to its scabbard, damascening

keenly drawn as his etched, eloquent ribs,
the cage that houses his likely offerings:
I am descended from a line of slaves.

My name in Sudanese means "pledged to live."
The reeds grow tall where Lake Kariba's waves
break. I cut and beat them. In Dinka they sing.

It Was a Normal Day Except I Fell

At 9:47 leaping, leaving the 108th floor, impressive
        to walk-up buddies,
    nothing quite like it in the Bronx:
Farewell, and 103rd floor, too, and there's Jerome, farewell,
    another scholarship kid;
On the elevator of public opinion, Raymond saying
    you're headed up, my man,
        up!
My own brother, who always sank the hook shot,
The back-home necks craning, tenements craning at my visits,
    my strides;

Farewell, 84th, and 54th, cell phones and land lines ringing,
    the whole hive on the hook with their homes,
        saying (I said it, too) *I love you, I'm okay,*
Farewell last words, preprogrammed at our unpacking,
    good taste in the mouth of survival,
        even the bullies found you.

Farewell, second-best khakis, the creases I love hardwired,
        constructive,
    under the dry cleaner's diaphanous hygiene,
And best of luck, closet, my secrets, my order:
Your cotton pinstripes ballooning and shrill

sing me down, whistle me,
   flap as I flap, pure folly,

Ah, the sky so blue, the sun in plain view, the cool
   silver siding, the heat inside—
I, no Icarus, no hubris, small pride in small mercies,
Farewell me, expanding like heat, my bones
Buckling, O Mother, O Father I never knew, O Love,
   what have we here?

Polar Bear in the Central Park Zoo

Watched, captivating, he swims to the rocky shelf
and berths a beat before pushing off with plate-sized
foot, belly up, yellow head plowing a watery furrow.

He soaks. A forepaw backstrokes the water once,
idly, but with force enough to speed his streamlined
bulk across the dole of open sea he's fathomed utterly.

He dives as if tethered, submerged body spread and flat
against the viewing glass, mounted momentarily, a trophy
hide on the lodge wall. Watchers shriek, but he moves on

his fixed orbit, water-logged planet, up to the rock, a push,
one backstroke, dive, eyes closed the while. His swim,
compulsory as a Busby Berkeley routine, has captivated

the bear, too, or made him half captive, while the other half,
repeating his invention move for move, seeks a different
outcome: a new mercy, colder, austere; more genuine ice.

Ivory-Billed Woodpecker

(As Identified by *The Audubon Guide:*
Small Land Birds)

I. EATING HABITS OF THE NEARLY EXTINCT

> *The ivory-bill's most important food is the larvae of*
> *wood-boring beetles, especially the flat-headed kind that*
> *work between the bark and wood of dying and newly*
> *dead trees. . . . As an ivory-bill will strip extensive*
> *areas of bark in a few feedings, it is most abundant*
> *where there has been an abnormal tree mortality because*
> *of fire, drought, wind, or insects.*

Louisiana, his grandmother, served stories for supper:
    of a shack in swampland, ham hocks
    on lucky days, firsthand sighting
    of a KKK blaze fighting the damp
    and losing, its keepers mopping
    their brows with sticky hoods.

And he dished out his:
    of extracurricular dissing, of Shaquina no more,
    of Killah Priest, whose rap has more stab
    than the canned laughter of a third-
        rate classroom
    where Miss Swift started fall full-voiced,
        got worn down to whispers;

of the hours watching sitcoms as she wept strangely,
        a class in break-dancing when she quit in May.

Now June turns his stomach in its six-foot frame, starves
        him down to one eighty-five, shakes
        his heart like Twista on the first track, *Kamikaze*
June, mordant June, the job-seeking month, the grubbing month:

First foldeth he his favorite red-hooded sweatshirt
        and tucketh it away,
Then press he his khakis himself, so the crease lay perfectly,
Then don he his Tommy Hilfiger shirt, XL with logo prominent,
And migrate him across bridges to maken eye contact.

No wind breaketh the sweat melting his crease, no fireworks
        herald his arrival as they did Killah Priest
        at the Nassau Coliseum (O Shaquina!),
On mail room and mail room, humming with health,
        he calleth
But none calleth him back, saying *come unto us, Mr. Reid,*
        who art the next Jay-Z,
        the next Notorious B.I.G.
No flat heads shed the hooded look of beetles
        when they are afraid to see, see here
        you worked at King Kullen. Didn't Ja Rule start there?
        And Lil' Flip in the corner store?
No one asks, a drought of questions, nothing
        to bore under his skin,

until one unappetizing insect on his fourth round:
How old are you anyway, Kent?
Fourteen. I'm only fourteen.

II. THE HABITATS OF SMALL LAND BIRDS

> *A normal, healthy forest has a low carrying capacity for*
> *ivory-bills. It is likely that most nesting has always*
> *been in "die-off" areas, since only these seem capable of*
> *providing enough flat-headed borers to feed a pair of*
> *adults and their brood.*

He lived B.I.G., his Brooklyn of ample hills in rubble;
The old growth brownstones were his high-rising hard
    woods in wilderness of double-parked cars;
The wino was his, asleep or dead, outside Pete's Tonsorial Parlor;
And the wino's arm flung across his eyes, crooked
    as a cypress knee;
Fort Greene Park, its mansions on the one side,
    projects on the other,
    its worlds facing off, his;
    its many stairs, its single stony tower.
Miz Ann's inadequate electric fan, satisfying
    fried chicken, his;
Popeye's 20-piece Bucket, also his;
His to never stray from, his river bottom,
    his boarding house.
His, not his.

His to be stopped, joyriding
In his grandmother's '72 Buick LeSabre,
    Kojak-brown;
His to be stopped in his red-hooded sweatshirt, the one
    Shaquina bestowed;
His to be stopped and questioned, stopped and searched,
        stopped
    and patted down, like bark stripped:
    Where were you Tuesday last?
    What's in the bag?
    Who you looking at?
    Let me see your registration, your license,
        your abs and glutes—

His to bench-press two hundred and fifty
    in the Audubon Society of Rikers,
    the Sierra Club of Corrections,
Where he will be Saved.

III. RANGE, AN ELEGY

> *Formerly the South Atlantic and Gulf States from s.e.*
> *North Carolina to e. Texas and up the Mississippi*
> *Valley to s. Illinois and Ohio. Also Cuba.*

All day long the television going, the weight room full,
    the library unopened,
The cinder-block day of tough, cheap, even, ugly,

thick-walled construction,
Each day stacked on the next like cells, the catwalks
    ferrying occupants' illusions of progress—
For the days stay the same, the chaos inside the day
    stays the same,
The body bulks, but the soul (O last prisoner out! O lifer!)
    stays small.

And the ivorybilled woodpecker is defiant,
In captivity he refuses all food,
Though large of size, charismatic of red,
He eludes sight.
He reck not the guidebook, the genealogical charts;
Indomitable he stays the course of his principles;
Though his forests lie fallen, yet will he not change
    his ways.
The ivorybill defieth, hero and victim of heroics,
He cresteth, and then no more.

IV. TERRITORIAL NEEDS, A LAMENT

> *Destruction of the vast forests of the South, has appar-*
> *ently doomed this splendid bird—largest of our woodpeck-*
> *ers. It is so rare that any record of one is noteworthy and*
> *should be passed on at once to the National Audubon*
> *Society, which is trying to save the bird from extinction.*

Woe is the last stand, the hot-headed pose, the cold blood
    of commerce,

The bravery of youth, the profit gathered in its wake.

Have I lamented the last stand of 1938, blaze and markings
    of the splendid bird's doom?
Lament I then:
First, the Singer Machine Company, seller of logging rights
    to certain Louisiana lands,
Second, the loggers, who must have the only trees left
for the ivorybill to live in, the old trees, the swamp lords,
Third, the witnesses, the bystanders, their comments,
        their safety,
Lastly, the ivorybill, the vivid folly of its flaming-red crest.

And protests appeared decrying the loss of habitat
        in newspapers made from trees,
And men in dungarees arrived with axes and saws
            whose day wages
        sustained them only till the trees came down,
And machines beetled into the humid depths
        fired by the impostrous gleam of fossil fuels,
And the naturalist sketched on his crooked knee,
And telegraph wires tapped impatient memos to headquarters
    along wooden poles planted all the way to New York:
        progress stop all clear except for bird stop,
For the lumberjacks were approaching the roosting tree,
            felling and felling,
        but the last known resident refused to fly.

And have I lamented another last stand, another
        splendid bird of the South?
Lament I then a boy of fourteen,
        a black boy of fourteen, 1944,
        a boy of distinction;
Lament I George Stinney of South Carolina:
        for his extinction is he remembered,
        for confessing the murders of two white girls
                is he remembered,
        at 95 pounds, so light for such dark deeds!
        at 5'1", so short, fourteen years!

For a sentence of death by electrocution is he remembered,
        for the carrying of it out on one so young
                is he remembered,
        the youngest American that century so killed.
(Foregone his conviction, scant information survives;
No newspapers hummed of George Stinney,
                asking questions.
A nesting pair of rumors was sighted: his family
        drummed out,
A small-town blaze near a swampland shack,
        no lawyer to decry and preserve,
and George Stinney alone in the Big House.)

Surely this is a misidentification:
        the mask falls off
        the boy is too small for it

black, white, red markings
jolt in the chair.

V. VOICE OF THE IVORY-BILLED WOODPECKER

> *A high-pitched, nuthatch-like note, clear and musical
> but plaintive. The call note sounds like* kent, *by which
> name the bird is sometimes known. The birds are not
> especially noisy, and their calls do not carry far.*

Hi my name is george I am
foreteen yrs old today fore
my birthday I got a pockit-
nife a nife for wittelling.

My pa is a witteller
he showd me how with
my nife I am going to make
a gun out of pine wood

to shoot birds thank you
Sometimes my mind goes
blank. I got a pockitnife.
the gun is not real jes the nife

VI. KNOWN PREDATORS

The ivory-bill has risen from the dead before. A nesting pair was found in Florida in 1924, at a time when naturalists considered the bird gone forever. The birds were shot and stuffed by hunters.

—Jonathan Rosen, "The Ghost Bird,"
The New Yorker, May 14, 2001

Taxidermist, ply thy arts! I lay this specimen upon the table:
The hunters brought it down, the last of its kind.
They could not resist the kill, it was so feral, so large, so full
    of fight.
They mean tenderly, the hunters.

And now I hang and cow, for I have not earned my life,
    nor have I hunted, tenderly,
    nor have I remonstrated with the hunters.
(I swear to you now I have wasted my youth and then some,
    in ways more forgettable than cinder blocks
    yet, with all my indolence, I am nowhere near extinct.)

This boy in his man's body, fierce body of a man,
    but fourteen years old—
I hope he has earned his years, which are to him a lifetime.
I see his abs peeled back, his great barrel chest—
The autopsy of my imagining reveals his heart:
    the adrenaline is gone, the movement, the grace,

the machinery flaccid
the bird raucous no more.

VII. Variations in Appearance

> Since the abundant and widely distributed pileated
> woodpecker is frequently mistaken for this rare bird,
> great care should be used in verifying its identity. The
> big, conspicuous, creamy-white bill and the white lower
> halves of the folded wings are its most notable charac-
> ters. In flight the rear half of the long inner wing is
> pure white.

Rare sightings filter back to us,
The anthropologist labors over documentation:
Look there! a mirage, a miracle! mistaken image of hope
    alive!

The bird falls to earth, a shadow, a myth:
    the myth of the black man, strong, doomed, valiant,
    the myth enduring though the man shot away,
    the myth enlarging, promoting boy to manhood
        before his time,
    keeps the ivorybill barely alive, to grapple
        the sackcloth
        of our sympathy:
Woe is make-believe, the big dream notorious,
Woe is the whittler of fake guns.

These matters of life and death, who can consider them
    in their habitat?
They are too elusive, their stealth masked by bravado.
Though we have searched, we are yet blind.
And in the wild, refusing all science, they expire into myth,
    feared extinct,
    feared,
    extinct.

Pecking Order

When mud runs clammy, the crows take control.
They carp from crabbed branches, dark clergy
    of the coruscant slime below.

Who's in charge they caw, craning over counterpane
    yards and gardens.
Their claws are ravenous for arms.

Expecting excalceations are they? or shrift from the rooked,
    the cowed, squab on black clay—
Black crows' scurfy echoes still convoke flocks.

Black uncanny wings, gathering.

From the Minister of Praise At Large

> *O Servant of God's holiest charge,*
> *The minister of praise at large,*
> *Which thou may'st now receive;*
> *From thy blessed mansion hail and hear,*
> *From topmost eminence appear*
> *To this the wreath I weave.*

> —*Christopher Smart, "A Song to David"*

STROLLING-OF-A-TUESDAY WOMAN

Winter completes her, dropcloth backdrop to her speck
    and splat.
From above she creeps as if on clean, white, slightly rumpled
    bedsheets under a microscope.
Close up, her boots flap. Her parka wheezes,
    a dowdy space suit
    or swaddling clothes.
She punches a trail in the newfangled snow.

On the golf course, among expensive drifts, her mittens
    prop her, first leftside, then aft.
She teeters with perspective, her position uncertain
    amid the whiteness.
Where did I go wrong?—yet she has gone this way
    before.

Not a soul in sight, not a soul answers her.

She is falling. No, she has righted herself. No, she is falling
    again, but on purpose.
The woman who takes long walks eases herself into gravity,
spills her momentous haunches onto a bank.

Prone, she rolls over, looks up into the cloudless console.
Her arms crank like an upturned beetle's,
her legs open and shut and open; she makes her angel
    in the snow.

THE MAN IN THE BLUE JANITOR'S PANTS

His shins, so thin he could shim a desk with them,
he sheathes in clean, black dress socks.
He has received a lifetime of multitudinous advice
    with grace:
Witness his hands, how gallant their tremor, receiving.

Once the people brought him down-home remedies:
    urine and nettles; now, upscale pills.
Um-huh, I'll surely try that, ice-cold, you say? magnets?
and thanks the doyen-slash-matron-slash-don, the latest
well-meaning captain of the white brigade.

The school is so private it barely has a name;

only a brass monogram someways in the corner;
thick carpet, thick glass, city shut out, books weighing in;

quiet seals of a remove barely disclosed to him.
Although nothing, nothing, in regular intervals, is given him
he tilts his head easy-like, as if reading Scripture.

SHE WHO SHEPHERDS THE STREET

You will not know her by her raiment, her Ladies Wear,
        her Good Brands.
She passes without comment in her adequate suit.
Her underwhelming midwaist bears up beneath, incarnate
        and getting heavier.
Who would touch her? Who would think to touch her?

You will not know her by her speech.
Her tongue does not twirl as Walt Whitman's twirls,
        encompassing worlds and worlds,
but burbles word-marbles, childish globes round and cursive
as the doodles of Mr. Krusch when he's not really listening.

You will not find her in office, for she lacks appointment.
She abides not with professionals whose corridors tap
        with wingtips.
Look to the common ways; look to plain sight that renders
        invisible;

There she goes, past the thin black couple in love, past
    concatenating bikes,
    past the wheelchair man.
She picks up half-empty clamshell cartons, leprous
    Wal-Mart sacks.
The song is in her heart, my friends. The song is in her heart.

THE THIRD-TO-THE-LEFT IN THE CAFETERIA

Macrosomatous over the cauldron in his smudgy white hat
he hulks, he slumps, defeated mascot of the giant spoon.
The mashed potatoes are smudgy, too, and sweaty as compost.
Everything wilts: sighing carrot jockey to the left of him,
    meatloaf lady, right;

The humidity deafens. Steam muffles the suck his potatoes
    make leaving his spoon,
the udder-like slap as they hit the pressboard tray on its forced
    march, the bearer soldier-faced.
They are reluctant succor, these mashed things, and disgusting,
    he knows.
He hunches more, ashamed.

The children fall silent before his great pot, his giant spoon,
    his bulk.
They duck their heads at the private suck and slap,
squishy potatoes scooped like breasts.

How he wishes he could shield these innocents from the deflating
    thought of potato, its lubberly heft, the batter of industry.
Then would his largeness be largess. He almost smiles, the shy one,
and the chubby shy child next in line almost smiles back.

THE POET WHO SITS ON THE SIDEWALK

By the end, in Camden, he never left the house but for nice
    spring days.
Then he'd be carried, wheelchair and all, to the sidewalk
and park'd there like a vet, begging for fresh air, for feet,
snatching at the pretty children as they went by.

And if he caught one, he'd work the boy onto his lap.
(This recollected by a friend, after his death: "Children
    loved him."
Not "The dirt receded before their prophetical screams.")
Walt Whitman held fast, hard on an indoor year,
    to his compassionating comrade

of five or six, and he'd tell a story, pouring out words;
he'd pour the words into the child's cochlea, listening
    for oceans,
the shock of contact turning him to speech.

And all the while his blood rushing and confused;
his blood thumping anthems: *I am here, use me! use me!*
but poems are gone, and only bedtime stories come.

Coyotes in Greenwich!

Here hedges are upholstered, each cobblestone
has an appointment, greening boughs aspire
in vain to Tudor style while even ramblers
know their place. And yet, we saw hibiscus
in high alarm, cat-slunk shivering it.

Coyotes invade. They claim to be the truth.
Black bears nose the bougainvillea, moving
eastward, indiscriminate, original.
Our sinks back up, our toilets will not drain,
our nature disobediently tends toward nature.

But we will have no blame, for we attend
our garbage as we always have, bury
and send away what could not prosper here.
In children's books we keep foxes and mice;
where are the Apaches to back us up?

Logically we sleep, though not in comfort
these days. Our wives keep turning in our beds
like roasting meat, the stones call out to us,
campfires fringe the Merritt. In our kitchens
pasta forks bare fangs, pans hang like scalps.

II

Archeology

The Visual Display of Quantitative Information

It's Valentine's, no time to window-gaze.
Across the way a woman leans westward,
smoking; another, two windows up and over,
steps back and shoulders her bag in one swift move.

Ready to go somewhere. And can they hear
the amateur saxophonist on the street
below, halting out "Moon River"? And can
they bear it? Valentine's, no time to practice.

No time for alacrity lacked on instruments.
I can stay angry for hours at a simmer,
explosive and chilly like an elaborate sauce.
The low sun flares up, glazing bricks to burnt orange,

windows to metal, then sinks as unambitious
browns assert themselves and rooms yield depths
to the sun's off-angle. Interiority
instructs me: turn on all the lights.

The saxophonist stumbles into the theme
from *The Odd Couple* and I swear to myself
I am not making this up. I will make up,
buy roses, call the office where your blinds

divulge through elegant Venetian slats
the fumarole: a Hudson lit to boiling
gold and, banking it, a Jersey kilned
adobe. Hues both poisonous and gorgeous.

Archaic Smile

I. Early Records

When you were little, my kouros, still safe inside the stone,
How I loved you and hoped you would not wear thick glasses,
    orthopedic shoes, correctives.
You were perfect to me then, not laughable.

And perfect as you played gladiator, wheezing *ahhh*
    for crowd noise,
Perfect, rounding third base toward home, already out,
    not realizing,
Perfect, sent to fetch a loaf of bread, returning with cat slung
    underarm like a loaf of bread,
Perfect, lost at a wake, disarranging flowers.

Then out you strode from boyhood, thrust into your characteristic
    pose,
    filled with movement but unable to move.
Exuberant One, who holds you back?
I would help if I could see the binding.
I would smite the hand across your chest.

(But I am only a mother, a distant point in time: how helpless
    are origins!)

Already your smile is Archaic,
     wise to exuberance.
You are out of date and know it.
The lips of your vessel, which have drunk honey,
     now release a drop,
As you do not flower into Classical grace.

Perhaps that will come later, after you,
After you are gone.

II. KOUROS

No credit here for gentle men, *Proceed down the hall*
in an orderly manner to Room B, Tragi-Comedy & Divorce.
You duck a grin, hot papers in your hand, must sign, must sign.

Obedience is pricey. So, too, an unstamped deed, defiance.
Your long feet pat toward the Bureau of Malfeasant Helpmeets,
where they punish the friendly for trying too hard, losing in battle.

Love, a weary captain, well trained and mortally wounded, you break
news right and left, your finest men speared on pikes or roped
neckwise. A brief smile in such moments, *It is required.* They fled

homes, like you. Amphora, krater, hydria, lekythos, kylix, oenochoe,
empty, left behind. Only a bracelet, perhaps, a clutch of blue stones.
Attributes held tightly as if they could indicate things, perceptions

of things. How you bleed, lightly, as if pleased! All of the vanquished
wind up somewhere. *Take a number*, odd if dead, even if alive.
If slightly chipped or soiled, *Remain seated, Do not move.*

Unlearn! you whisper to one young soldier, spare yourself rules!
The boy stays put, his future already punctuated, a point so fine
it might as well disappear like everything else. The dismantling
                                                              begins.

Dear God, all along you knew you'd be sacked. Some chiseler
made you, some Persian unmade you, same as everyone else.
That's the joke. All along, you knew you'd never be loved.

III. KORE LOST, REDISCOVERED NEARBY

Chiefly of interest is the drape, also the color
mixed with wax applied while hot. All dead stone
has been carved away, the girl is freestanding.
Her ankles are broken. She is wearing your smile.

IV. UNTRANSLATABLE GLYPH

This is what is not known:
How you worked in that sales job for that awful man—
A vole, betraying his genus with bad shoes, bad smell,
        necrotizing personality,

Hate everywhere, its pressure turning you to stone.

Not known: once coming home unarmed, soldier
        in a cardboard box,
The door fighting your push, the door jammed,
        you swearing at dead weight everywhere,
Then the resentful opening, the *shush* of junk mail, the weight
        revealed:
Rumpus, your cat, his cold fur attached to stone,
Rumpus, who quit without mentioning it.
My, my, this job is killing me.

V. Archeological Digs

May she wither to a footnote in the pressure of centuries,
May ill repute visit her in smashes
        and the hammer of appraisal spare her not.
May she become as hearsay, intangible and misunderstood,
May her stone flesh rot like fish, her face rut like the bones of fish,
May the bits of her be then flung seaward, irretrievable and sand-
                                                    making.
May her voice never again gush forth as hair, or as sunlight,
May darkness fall upon her charms as if a knife in the hand
        of rumormongers
May she not last, no, nor thrive.

VI. Art History 101

See, here in Chapter Three you are considered!
See, you are not utterly rejected.
My son, I turn a page and there you are, impressing
    upon me that half smile,
Is it fading? brightening?
Is it remorse for her gaze, false and fragile?

I was never sure what you were for, my son, except to suffer,
    not new enough to learn.
There you are, before love and after,
Anticipating folly and powerless against it,
Resurfacing in textbooks, where your archaic smile
    is dubbed "so-called,"
As if you hadn't meant it at all,
As if—surely you'd agree—it were some kind of mistake.

Now that I am long dead, longer than you, I take no joy
    from these excavations.
Everything is backwards.
How gentle you were at first, how short your life, how enduring
                      your burial.
I fired you in love's kiln, love's granite finished you.

Valediction

The air does not tingle and fume with his love.
A creak of stair tells me nothing.
No affinity seizes me, palm print from the hall
    door knob
so responsibly reflected by the mirror.

The gleam of polish on the hardwood
floor is gleam of polish and no more,
not caring to suggest dress shoes shined
    by a zealot
in somewhere's closet, perfectly aligned.

Good-bye. It's inarticulate, yet jointed, tongue in groove,
his return mere theory, quite unlike my hand
on the banister, one foot straightening
    a throw rug,
quite unlike forgetting why I came upstairs.

Pine Cone, Fallen

How gray you look now, little top, outlavished
by marigolds; how squat and wooden,

invisible within your tarnished armor.
Around you blades of grass, gay rapscallions.

Snakes do what you do: sneak geometry
beneath the notice of boughs, skirt their strikes

in unassuming poses. Seeds you spit
as poison, modestly. I see you've opened

at last: I love you for it, hail you, junk
bloom, shingled stone. Winter's lurking somewhere,

and shades will rise out of you, shuddering
like iron bridges to a sun you never ruled.

Mercy School

ESSAY ONE: TWELVE STEPS

> *Begin by sitting together in quiet for a few minutes. It's*
> *a good idea to hold hands. You will need to shelve your*
> *ego and invite your witnessing capacity to be present.*

> —Drs. Evelyn and Paul Moschetta

This ringed hand, then: take it before it tugs
on its last shirt, vee at the neck to mark
the pheasant you once were, game to trail ditches
brazenly. Fold this hand in that pyrite wing,
which hides itself as only memory hides,
under goldfleck, spangled green, bright russet.

These few weeks have mown their long grass down.
I haul my bones over ruts and roots to the gully
where you, my young self, nests. Your beak tufts chaff
and slough. You've found a use for your elder selves
their agons of molt, their bearing scythes, their loss
of heat and down, small feathers that draw wolf.

What collar and cassock wait in a private room
where singing lessons take their pornographic
turns? Arpeggios and Vaseline:

to be holy is to be available.
That fourteenth fall, your trousers mortally stained,
you hid your troubles in a bicycle wreck:

iridescent twists of green, gold, chrome,
your blood bright russet, pants in venial shreds.
Your mother won't believe you, so you held
small faith in intercession. Football season
benched, you backfired time for *amoroso*
to spare, for *practice! today's another lesson.*

Shelve your ego, your good idea. Invite
no witnesses until they've died and you
can see your way to follow them through cobwebs
and dew, the susurration of goldenrod, ragweed,
lamb's-quarters; until the devil's paintbrush leaves
you flushed, a pheasant, plume shot with copper.

ESSAY TWO: MEDITATION

> *Pathways Four through Six are particulary helpful in
> learning to live in the eternal now moment, although all
> of the Pathways reprogram you to tune in to the now-
> ness of your life.*
>
> —Ken Keyes, Jr.

I am Orpheus in boxers, no longer
waiting for reprieve, revision

of my fatal glance, but not yet singing.
What was it I lost? No matter, I am
recovered, as a casket is recovered—

remember the hallfull of Gothic sarcophagi
cloistered in Brugge? Restorationists chalked
white outlines, a rochet's gold orphreys, a miter,
a crime scene of clergy leaning in limestone
repose, remember? I want to go back—

to come back as a casket recovered
after the looters are done.

Essay Three: Primal Scream

Your are now ready for the crucial step in mood trans-
formation—substituting a more rational, less upsetting
thought in the right-hand column.

—David D. Burns, MD

Be your own loving parent.

—Drs. Evelyn and Paul Moschetta

I could never tell her anything,
but I could smell her dying
from the ogee windows of Notre Dame:

when she tried to say *ambulance*,
it came out *cantaloupe*.
Before long she'd mislaid her name

and the fact that she was my mother.
Then train travel, radiator painted over
a thousand times, books and camphor.

Cedar chest with buffalo nickels couched
in cashmere, Dad's illiterate love letters, a séance
one time at my best professor's house.

His Victorian den was decked in antlers.
Busts of composers jammed into corners.
A stuffed pheasant ran the mantle.

There were no messages, only the tin
ear of disappointment,
as with Yeats and automatic writing,

Merrill's ouija, the best minds of generations,
uneasy in their old dispensations,
turning to faddish blather. I was not taken in,

and looked no more for eleemosynary relief
from that century's skeptical gods. Grief
school is out, I said. I'll get my flapdoodle

from an Institute: daily Mass, where I go furtively,
ashamed to have forgiven already
my confessor. Mercy school is in. All my money

I gave to tradition. Kyrie Eleison, Christe
Eleison, Kyrie Eleison.
To be holy is to be empty.

Essay Four: Mantra

> *As you gain insight into the Cornucopia Center of
> Consciousness, you will begin to feel that you live in a
> friendly world that will always give you 'enough'
> when you live in the higher centers of consciousness. You
> will also begin to deeply feel that you live in a* perfect
> *world.*
>
> —Ken Keyes, Jr.

My daughter does not regard me, that my hair
has molted, my marriages rot on the flower dump.

She has her own child who chatters when she phones
to chat, thick in the mat and weave of roadsides.

I sheltered you, I want to say. *I followed all the pointers
to this end.* She cheeps and settles while I do no harm,

a mercy, a wooden handle on an old washtub
that dents in A–flat when you drag it along.

Sonnet: To a Marriage That Cannot Be Saved by a Weekend in Calistoga

Like the worming in, the mudbath clasping,
too close, the forced wallow and float, revolting
flecks, dermatic shreds. Like ginseng molting
in tea, oppression's hot wet fecal grasping.

Or worse, oppression's aftermath. The prickle
left when you've brushed a spider from your lip.
Insect scurry, low-volt, eight-point grips
you swear have colonized you knuckle to ankle.

Shudderful, the opposite of clean.
A cast-iron claw-foot tub, but light and charmless.
A racist joke. Too much, not enough,

the weak twine of a contradiction, the stuff
of truancy. And worst of all, harmless:
that anguish of not saying what you mean.

Hate Poem

I hate you truly. Truly I do.
Everything about me hates everything about you.
The flick of my wrist hates you.
The way I hold my pencil hates you.
The sound made by my tiniest bones were they trapped
      in the jaws of a moray eel hates you.
Each corpuscle singing in its capillary hates you.

Look out! Fore! I hate you.

The blue-green jewel of sock lint I'm digging
      from under my third toenail, left foot, hates you.
The history of this keychain hates you.
My sigh in the background as you explain relational databases
      hates you.
The goldfish of my genius hates you.
My aorta hates you. Also my ancestors.

A closed window is both a closed window and an obvious
      symbol of how I hate you.

My voice curt as a hairshirt: hate.
My hesitation when you invite me for a drive: hate.
My pleasant "good morning": hate.

You know how when I'm sleepy I nuzzle my head
        under your arm? Hate.
The whites of my target-eyes articulate hate. My wit
        practices it.
My breasts relaxing in their holster from morning
        to night hate you.
Layers of hate, a parfait.
Hours after our latest row, brandishing the sharp glee of hate,
I dissect you cell by cell, so that I might hate each one
        individually and at leisure.
My lungs, duplicitous twins, expand with the utter validity
        of my hate, which can never have enough of you,
Breathlessly, like two idealists in a broken submarine.

Gifted

Gifted in humor, that crossroad of crooked back
      streets I never realized meet right here,
Gifted with intensity, knitted of brow, determined as a quilt,
Gifted in logic whip-stitched to zeal, talent for piecing
      and worry,
Giftedly dramatic, gestural, accumulations laid out and cast
      wide, passionate as a unified theory of history,
Gifted of touch, of itch, of desire, the saline and crystalline
      reduced to tears.
Hot steam rises from his drawn-up knees.

Stray

For I will consider my Cat, Red Dog,
So named of the Following Categories: Red and Dog.
For he was born Red of fur and disposition.
For though not a Dog, he disporteth himself as One.
And trifling as paw to yarn, and loyal as tongue to tunafish,
He is mine as much as he is not,
That is, he belongeth to the grass, as I do,
And to the stream of air.
When taking it in or weaving through it, his shoulder blades
     rut the breeze as plowshares.
And he belongeth to the General Category of Lost,
     as I do.

For Red Dog, he did wander by
     but he did wander away.

We thought there'd be a prophecy, or at least
a pamphlet, mimeographed and hung
child-high on trees. Why no random heralds
for Him who came at Random, blown like litter,
caterwauling? Thus we looked for signs,
though found we none. A universe obstinate
and ambiguous, our moral noses not keen,
we feared to keep him. We let stray be stray.

For Red Dog, he did wander by
     and he did wander away.

The last time I saw Red Dog, that very day
There did arrive a bottle-fly blue pickup truck,
     Specific Category Hot Rod,
Abundant in cubic inches enough to crush a cat,
Wheels doubled up & high, very clean, Large & Category Invention
Driver drifting over the purr, thoughts of Personal
     Recreation Devices,
Slapper of aftershave, ears full of Heavy Metal, Red Neck,
     a brother of cats under his skin.

Let stray be stray, you counseled me, smell of her
     cutting your beard.

And Red Dog, he did wander by
     but he did wander away.

An errant driver in his big cat came,
Post hoc, ergo propter hoc you vanished Fallaciously:
This much I know, who has no proof, no body,
Only the stroking feel of conviction about my ankle.
I occupy the Sidelong Category Disposed Of,
     and Red Dog, too,
With Stung, a chapped pink cheek,
And absence, that Saucy Knave,
     that hot salt.

74

Sonnet: On a Recurring Argument Going Nowhere

The red-eyed gas gauge glares: attend! attend!
but you insist we're nowhere near empty.
We taxi past Texacos, bypass BPs,
our engine inventing fuel, me at wit's end,

you fuming at my lack of confidence.
We pause at last, a Shell somewhere in Jersey
not to fill up, but just to buy some candy.
By now I've hit the interstate of silence,

the pissed-off lane, the sullen bend, the unsound
skids and brakes. I ponder where to go
the next chance I can take sabbatical.

The car konks out. Stillness emphatical.
I've never much complained of breaking down
until today. Guess what: I told you so.

III

Fine Print

Loose Leaf from a Destroyed Journal

To my knowledge, she never scrapped any of her poetic efforts.

—Ted Hughes

In my dream's dream
I rake the flood, toiling in molten gold streams
of leaves, leaves by the ream.

I can't keep up with fall.
Red words drop, I sweat, they drop fireballs
onto bonfires tall, as tall

as Babel. Inklings, they're kindling, they're towers
building hour by hour
as bleeding trees see fit. If lit, what powers

could smother them? They'd usher in a new Dark Age:
December, brown and sage.
Pages—rusted poems, scrawled, sprawled foliage

dumped a fathom
deep—they burn, they burn. Losing, I fought them
hard in the autumn

of my dream.
Now silvery, like the script of a frozen stream,
they whiten, love. They scream.

Dependent Clause

How at the end of dinner, when we're glutted
but still anxious from having eaten out
(Fifteen-dollar eggplant! Juice, three bucks!
Who *picked* this hot-shot pasta shop?)

and then the bill comes in its precious sleeve
of briefcase brown, a padded dossier
as if it were the floor plan to a top-
secret U.S. military plant

for killer germs or stealth-type zapper rays
and we were comrades in one coherent cell,
"Well," you push back in your easy chair,
the only one among us with a house

in the Hamptons, plus a pure-bred Weimaraner
you've named Gide and use to mesmerize
the girls you dump once they've become attached
if not to you then to your high-toned dog,

"Well," you say, your kissy British accent
getting kissier as you draw your wallet,
"I had the salad, seven ninety-five"
and sliding two fins alongside your calamari

("For the table, shall we?"), Perrier
(three-fifty) and New York tapwater (free,
but you insist on lemon) you depart us,
saying how it's been a privilege.

Sonnet: Upon Losing One's Lease, the Devastation Thereof

All's bare since belted Ivan and chunky Juan
have trundled sofas, chairs and double bed
downstairs where bookshelves dissemble. Already gone
the giveaways, throwaways, junked, scrapped, shed—

only I remain, and the rug, its shadows
of furnishings the vacuum memorized.
What dust mouse dormed so faintly here who had those
things arranged thus, the emptiness disguised?

Now I can dwell here immaterially,
and prop my feet on the thought alone of matter,
(a prerogative of being mostly dead)

and someways in the corner there's a smatter
of small talk, and the bulky bureau of unsaid
laundry: O Ivan, O Juan, I am here! Move me!

Coney Island

I. AERIAL VIEW

A top spins over the field of poetry, right here
    on the boardwalk!

Narrative, a Russian couple clad in weedy black stroll
    and smoke deeply.
They are considering something together.

Trailing them, the first generation, a teenage couple,
    two miserable revisions offsprung
    in black imitation leather pants
keep distance, the measure of shame.

Postmodern Manhattanites, clad in ironic black, also "stroll"
    "here" and "smoke,"
Aspiring to consideration, which is always ahead of them
    deep in conversation.

One loosened page of a Korean newspaper wheels
    lyrically, toward the illegible sea—

The pastoral sands amuse themselves with shape,
    the out-of-town mother unpacking picnic.
The air is salty and ripe with Wu–Tang Clan, fat girls
    on cell phones, teenagers groping.
This was not what she expected.
Her child has found a balloon, a condom balloon,
    and frolics.
Baloney and pickle sweat in her hand.

Confessional, the Bowery, Arcadian arcade
    booth worn thin by the off-season,
    paint a weathered spiel, signs barking
Shoot the Freak. 3 Darts $5. Show, Don't Tell.

A boy in a red sweatshirt steps right up
    into the confessional
Poet's coffee break with Romanticism, retired mobster
    who lives in the projects nearby.
The mobster's leaning in, *Trust me, I got a feel for this—*
Sweatshirt misses.
Too bad, Confessional Booth Man says with manufactured
    sincerity. *Better luck next time.*
Booth Man's father shot himself one hot day in Deadwood.
    Hey kid, I'll make you a deal.
    Three darts for five dollars.

II. Concessions

The poem of soft ice cream melts baby fat and baby smiles
    down the Promenade,
Poem of a middle-aged pervert sunning on a park bench
    exposing himself, a stiffening I.
Before him a top spins, potent, attractive, manipulative—
    like the onion domes of tsars
    borrowing their force.
The top has stars on it, painted in gold so old it's exotic.

A mother pushes an empty stroller, her little boy afoot
    and not yet spying the top.
They came from carousel, deathtrap baited with gilt
    rose and purple and Pop
    Goes the Weasel,
From the clatter shadow of Wonder Wheel and Cyclone.
The mother smiles; her stroller was not stolen.
The ticket lady had said it would be okay
    and it was
    okay.

The poem of the pervert smiles, too, and gazes at the top
    as if gazing at a top,
Sits too still, poised and mathematically impossible,
    a quarter that ought to drop off the ledge.

The poem of the top spins like cotton candy.

The poem of the pervert gathers, hustles, tugs,
    pulls the child like taffy—
The mother pulls her child away, taffy at his spread thighs,
The poem, sunning itself in the naked light, moves.

A mother whirls, a smile wobbles, a top relaxes
    its orbit, satisfaction penetrates the instant.
Her face twists, Cyclonically.
In the toying with her vigilance,
The poem has been glimpsed, and that is enough for the poem.

III. EULOGY FOR JOHN MCKANE, CZAR OF CONEY ISLAND (1840–1899)

We are gathered here to remember John McKane,
Who was not an alcoholic, let it be said, nor a Catholic
But a leading citizen and member of the body politic
Until he became a corpse. And this, his last campaign,

We remember as well: how he breathed life insurance
Into the pocketbooks of Mermaid Avenue, and Neptune, and
                           Bowery,
So that, for a modest premium, every fine old lady
Could afford to die. Yes, a monument to endurance

And enterprise, Our John, for we remember also how he was only
                        just released

From Sing Sing, where he'd resided of late,
In a seclusion uncharacteristic of our foremost magistrate,
      ballot-box stuffer, kickback taker, rent raiser, and all-around
                Kingsborough *eminence greased.*

We remember the gold lining from his years of public service,
How it glistened like the Mighty Atlantic, glowed like the sand.
Shifted like the sand, too. There was something underhanded
About that gold lining. It never felt solid, like building on ice

While the Atlantic sucks the value right out of your floe here
Where desire, like water, is always much larger than the take,
And no reformer, Investigatory Committee or grand jury can slake
Desire, my friend, or as John put it, *Injunctions don't go here.*

This is Coney Island, 1899. Why stop at gold? at Sing Sing? at
                    Right and Wrong?
Remember John McKane! No matter how stuffed your mattress,
Don't stop until you cash in your pulse. The readiness
Is all or nothing! When this stiff century turns, I hope it's still
                    stringing me along.

IV. HOT DOG INVENTED, 1868 (IN THE HIP-HOP STYLE)

You've been hustling for centuries
    little spit
    sand thumb

screwing, grubbing, cheating at dice till dumb
        luck had nothing to do with you
Pickpocket, pocket liner, padded bill,
        flinting finger in the till
        of every Lunatic Steeplechasing dreaming
                Dreamland
        this side of Gravesend

You've been ratting out the Dutch, taxing religious nuts
        flacking for Our Lady of the Unsuspecting Putz
Even the locals been flimflammed

Remember the Canarsies? Fine folk
        mowed down by Mohawks
        for not paying up—
(I'm paid up and shook down
        hoodwinked evening gowned
shimmied and whored
        lease breaker to your slumlord

You can't fire me, lover, I quit:
Nobody tells me when to split,
Least of all no how-long low-down habit
        I been gambling
                to break
Truth on speed, what bleed, it bleed,
but blood is just some makeup on the tart cheek
        of greed)

Hip hop you can't stop your con
     no matter how high the heat is on
You're Coney: phony testimony
     libel, defamation
Doorstop to The Fifty States of Exploitation

V. The Top's Perspective

Reduced to physics, man's inhumanity
to man is optical illusion, a gamble
on pattern. Take a guess: I'm striped. Ha. Double
or nothing. I'm starred. I gotcha. To toy with me,
that's physics; to think you toy with me, well, that's
philosophy. Meanwhile, who gave you your weekend
gift for luck? I'm still here, Monday's freak, when
the con game you call confidence falls flat.
Will you feel had, then? Don't. It's all one, Number
Twenty-nine tonight, dear Mark, deceit
is spelled in zeros and atoms, there's no refuge.
Sunsets explained are drained of their feinting amber.
Just know the world's not spinning on its feet:
You are. It's centrifuge, not subterfuge.

VI. Fine Print at the Bottom of the Contract

Whereas: the aforesaid boy shall estop his toddle,
Whereas: the top, heretofore referred to as "Top," shall spin,
The interested party shall claim her property without prejudice.

Coney Island hereby agrees that nineteen percent of Americans
believe they are among the wealthiest one percent.

Coney Island hereby likes its chances on the Tilt-A-Whirl.

Coney Island hereby enjoins Rudy's Bar and Grill to be Open.

Coney Island hereby avers, *I thought he said five dollars for the whole
thing, I didn't think it would be five dollars apiece.*

Coney Island hereby translates pleasure into the brattling risk
of a construction zone.

Coney Island hereby goes *shut up, shut up, shut up. No you
shut up.*

Coney Island hereby underwrites the homeless guy with the blue
stuffed animal.

Coney Island on the loudspeaker hereby proclaims:
     Slow down, everybody wait your turn

Slow down, everybody wait your turn
Slow down, everybody wait your turn
Hey, I said no pushing down dere!

Coney Island hereby debates whether seawater stays the same level
or gets higher and lower. That reminds me, there's a leak in the sink.

Coney Island hereby has faith in the Right to Life and Death
                                                    Penalty.

Coney Island hereby proffers the nub of illusion, love
of illusion, everybody tricked but me, but me.

Everybody tricked but me.

I Am Not a Confessional Poet

There I was, someplace in Westchester, reading,
and there they were, the people of Westchester, listening.
After I'd read some poems, I sat down. After other,
better poets read other, better poems, everybody mingled.

There was a platoon of white wine in glass, not plastic
stemware, flanking an attractive spread of cheeses marred
only by the tough-talking but ultimately chinless
character of club crackers, which tend to crumble

at even pliant cheeses like brie and camembert. Normally,
I am not a Confessional Poet, nor do I write confessionally,
but as I mingled, a man homed in on the really terrific poet
to whom I'd cleaved just as she spun away, Daphnesque,

to a dubious fate. The man, an expert on body language,
was left with me. Naturally, his body began to chat, saying,
"I would rather be talking to that more brilliant poet
over by the lunch-meat and tortilla pinwheels."

As you know, I am not a Confessional Poet, but I was
curious whether my body confessed anything of interest,
such as "I would never appear on *Oprah*." Perhaps
my physique expressed itself in charm or aphorism:

"Trust grows inversely to speed of communication,"
it might say, somewhat grandly, and let slip I've read
all of Jorie Graham's work and am keen to read more.
Instead, he scanned my nonce form, dactyl to foot, en-

jambed right down to my feminine ending, and pronounced
me as saying: "I am hidden." Did I mention that I am not a

Confessional

Poet? Nor do I write confessionally, but I did get told
on once, in Westchester. Someone absolved me there.

Untenable Position of His Mother-in-Law

The plane's airless whine announces your arrival, but they don't hear
    it, they don't greet you,
Just as you don't hear their consternation, your daughter's quick
    inhale
      held too long, the low "this is it, John."
God, when she was young she was misguided, always
    pulling on dangerous levers, sucking her dirty fist,
      balled up in unlikely places—hampers, stairwells, crawl
        spaces.
After dinners she'd lie down on the rug, accustomed to a spot
    no one else would have chosen.

You can't hear a thing upon landing, neither grunge
    nor clamor affects you.
"This is it," she was saying at that very moment. "This is it."
God, her first apartment was a firetrap, hellhole, rat's nest,
    and her second, and her third.
"This is it," pulling up to another hazard, always
    pulling up to risk like an illegal parking spot
    in a dicey neighborhood.

You can't hear the tightening, the muscle, the cramp,
So that by the time you pull up to your daughter's apartment
    she's in the delivery room

Along with that husband of hers on his cell phone,
     not paying attention.
You never say a word, but he hates you anyway.
You smell it, judgment, just as he smells yours.

Fugitive

*In June of 1999, FBI agents and police in St. Paul,
Minnesota, surrounded a Plymouth Voyager minivan
containing a suburban mom named Sara Jane Olson.
The woman later admitted that she was actually
Kathleen Ann Soliah, former member of the Symbionese
Liberation Army. She eventually pled guilty to conspiracy
to commit murder for her part in a 1975 attempted pipe
bombing of two police cars and went to prison.*

Under the hum of nervous wires circling the freezer
    it lies:
suspended in the lint it makes up,
too small to do anything but leap like static to doorknobs.

Lacking all sound, it hovers: phantom item
on the list of things to pick up in town.
Even the tick of an electric clock has more enunciation.

Still, it's why I breathe, and why at night, asleep, I die
    provisional deaths.
It watches, it tightens, I wind up, knowing it is alive—

Deadwood, S.D.

Imagination's horse trader is childhood:
for a scrap of curtain, coronations bloom.
Toy kings flourish even in two-bar towns
where only windows dressed as royals should.

But who got bartered back there? A hogherd's son
who thought his switch was scepter, for a suit,
and daughters in casinos making change,
not hay, for favors not in kind but coin.

Old women reign in Deadwood now. The men
have left their honeysuckle sows for yields
of telemarketing. The curtains hang.

Queens hoe hardscrabble plots swathed in hodden,
picking out kernels from exhausted fields
spread, as curtains, for privacy or shame.

Rural Development News

(As Reported in "Dimensions of the Rural
Population," by Willis Goudy)

> *Three subdivisions of the rural population—farm, town,*
> *and country residents—have fared quite differently*
> *during recent decades. . . . One trend is obvious to*
> *observers of the rural North Central region; the farm*
> *population has declined dramatically during the 50*
> *years from 1940 to 1990.*

My rental car parks at Hard Luck and Hardship,
glinting like a city, frosty and silver, upholstered
in urbane denial of gravel. It's a brusque little Ford Focus

and says "where the fuck *are* we?" But I am not lost,
not even after twenty years of freeway.
I had only forgotten how much dust there could be,

and trouble by the ruck, and rubbly skin, cement, rained-on
plastic trikes, and cement-block houses painted the pink
of rained-on plastic trikes, as if the unanimity of this slow fade

could coat poverty. This is a town? This is a town
of woe, and I am not lost, only revisiting. Here is my own house
no longer mine except in the olive-green shag of memory,

where it remains clapboard. Some newer owner
has rehabilitated it, has gussied it up in slick molded-plastic
siding the color of frozen mud, a bid to make endurance

look easier. My old house now gleams like Styrofoam
peanuts packing collectible plates that commemorate
the 4-H Club. It is a house shellacked, dreaming no more

of paint, hammer, spackle or sanding, of Head, Hands,
Heart or Health. Memory is subsidy, propping up
a has-been haggle of fact for unprofitable dream.

> *The second trend involves small towns and it is con-*
> *trary to many images held about what has occurred in*
> *this portion of the rural population. About 4.1 million*
> *people lived in rural towns in the Midwest in 1940.*
> *Fifty years later, nearly the same number was noted for*
> *such towns.*

Contrary to image, I did not park at Hard Luck and Hardship.
In my childhood, these streets, too few to remember, had no names.
But illusions of change moved the town planners to plant Elm,
Maple and Main, a spatter of numbers, 1st Street through 6th.

There they are, the signs of progress, tracking all twenty-four blocks
of barren road. A lone stoplight blinks in confusion:
"Where on God's green earth *am* I?" My sarcastic car hums
to the omnivorous silence an utter lack of traffic generates.

When I was a child. When I was a child. When I was a child
spring replaced storm windows with screens held by wing nuts
and robin's-egg blue was the Windex we used
to scrub off the winter before stowing bad weather

in the garage where the heavy wood frames sat all summer,
paint in a state of peel, putty cracked and pulled from the panes,
leaning in rows: old LPs in a record bin, old maps in Pageant
Bookstore, now defunct, old shingles on a saltbox, 1847.

Contrary to image, there is no obsolescence here. I mislead.
The house today is hung with Anderson windows,
All-weather aluminum, too small to let in much light.
Only memory lets in light, bounteous light, and bushel baskets

for leaves, swept linoleum, canna bulbs gathered before the frost
in paper bags we saved from Mr. Brown's grocery, long out
of business, as well it should be, contrary to image. Inside the house,
consumers shelve their packaged goods from the supermarket

where they work now, forty miles yon, over the county blacktop.
"Some benefits, decent pay," say their Chevy Cavaliers. "These colors
don't run." Writers write. Commuters commute. Poets waste
their lives. A house is for bedrooms, as if in Milwaukee.

And so, contrary to image, this house is as full as it ever was,
though it demands no labor of its sleepers: no 4-H, no putty,

no remembrance laying its dust thick to build shape, to make darkness visible, no coat of old paint, no tattered frame.

> *One trend hasn't been recognized to the extent that it deserves. It involves the remainder of the rural population —those not living on farms or in small towns. This segment—called country residents here—accounted for less than one in five of all rural residents in 1940, but more than three in five in 1990 in the Midwest. Country residents include several types, such as those occupying housing units that formerly were the homes of farm residents, those living in housing developments outside of incorporated places, and those building homes on acreages that have aesthetic amenities frequently associated with rural life, such as overlooking a river valley or in part of a forested area.*

In pursuit of aesthetic amenities, I went to college, got a credit card, and now can rent a car.

My schoolmates, self-reliant farmers' sons, cashed their federal checks until they could sell off the workings as scenery, a harmless reversion frequently associated with rural life.

Country residents translate millpower and watering trough, compost and dumping ground into a fine view from a house they occupy like hermit crabs.

And who can blame the aboriginals their disposals, their bum
shells, their turns toward Mr. Scrappy, and Corningware over corn,
which doesn't pay at $3 a bushel?

Poetry is the only obsolescence, wishing itself away in revisitations
of unsentimental haunts, scuttling across the treadmarks Chevrolets

leave

so cavalierly behind.

Ghazal: Orient Point

The right whales went wrong, from capitalism's viewpoint.
A lighthouse stands corrected, obsolete but sturdy (to a point).

Fetch me a wooden sailor perched on a whittled boat, bobbing for
Luck. Fetch a diminishment of what once rounded Orient Point.

Those old New England towns grow indigents, unoriginal trees
Living on the lyrics to old sea shanties worked in needlepoint.

I pry you like a barnacle from the hull of serenity. My stillness,
You've slept through another journey to an eastern point.

You wear your white fishing cap low as if it had no brim. I know
It's love, that sidestepping afterthought, mislaid and always off-point.

Thoreau is shouting again: awake! To the mast! Reorient
Yourself! The hour wrecks, it sinks, for time honors no distant point.

Today I harvest. Tomato plants. String beans hidden, wishful.
My marriage, a colander. Dill, green hymn. To wash, a counterpoint.

Our towering quarrel withstands high wind, lash of couplets, broken
lines, fresh news. O the folly of shining at starpoint or gunpoint!

Summer revives to poison itself, as if it had green to spare.
Why does the wild month of Julie dwell so long on Orient Point?

IV

Catalogues

Candling Eggs

It was just a job. You sit at the conveyor belt while
eggs jounce one after another through a warehouse
lit only by candles. Just a job, but sepia-toned

like the flashback scenes in the TV movie that got you
through last night. Each egg a tiny starlet, white
and slightly out of focus, drawing the light to herself

as starlets do. Arrayed on either side, adoring fans,
plainswomen who hunch and search, eyes sweeping.
You work swiftly, plucking eggs from the tumble,

gather as many in each hand as you can grasp
without breaking, and, lifting them upward, offer them
to the candlelight, turning them this way and that—

priestesses, big boned but deft. Candlers. *I was one
of those.* Looking for flaws, that was the job. Coaxing
secrets out of those manicured shells. Eggs impregnable

as the owner's wife with her perfect nails, headscarf
a varnish on her platinum hairdo—until you get them
up to the light. Then you see what's what: red yolks,

blood spots, cracks, the ones already fertilized showing
at last the first embryonic curl of life. These must be
destroyed. That was the job. The candlelight treacherous,

beautiful. The women, dingy ghosts at a séance, gleaners
of horrors, experts in how shadows will describe and then
betray the creatures that cast them only to cast them out.

Detection, that was the job. Destruction. You break the eggs
that won't make it to the afterlife of their consumption.
Some women liked that part. Not you, single, childless, your first

in the oven. All gone now, the produce trucks, warehouse,
farmhands in their overalls. Even the bars, their bluish gleam
that played along the alley of a Midwestern town exotically

named LeMars. *I could lift eight eggs at a time.* You lift
your glass, as if to demonstrate, fingers haloed like tapers
in oracular crimson, beer the hearty gold of candlelight.

St. Philomena

The bones of a fourteen-year-old—*Madonna mia,*
what could she have possibly done at that age
      warranting martyrdom,
nobody knows. *Gallina vecchia fa buon brodo,* besides
she was still a virgin, if the iconography can be believed.

They found a glass vial; inside, the brownish remains
of blood. Also drawings: two anchors, three arrows,
      a palm. *Che cazzo!*
Naturally we assumed the usual—a virgin, a martyr,
a Christian, death by gruesome means, the girl demented

with holiness, *vacca miseria,* though no doubt
she didn't feel a thing. That's how the female ones
      manage it: ecstasy
pitched to pain in a kind of polarization of sense.
Ah, she suffered gladly, did Philomena—

if indeed those bones *are* Philomena's: there's some question
of the tiles that sealed the grave, inscribed "Go in peace,
      Philomena" (hence the dead girl's name),
having been moved there from some *other* Philomena's
final resting place. *Prendere due piccioni con una fava,*

I always say. But what a waste of piety if these bones
belonged to some common thing, a whore, even, a leper,
    puttana la Madonna, a servant!
Wouldn't that be rich, me in my best robes, greeting the faithful
on her feast day, displaying her relics with utmost care,

porco Dio, I might as well be peddling pigs' bones!
Well, what does it matter? What does all of this incense
    and indulgence matter?
Belief—it's nothing compared to the glamorous
undertow, the tug of violence at the vortex of faith.

Va bene, then, the cult persists. Viva Philomena.
    How small our gods have become.

Harriet Tubman

Lights out at nine, Mother says. It's nine-ish
but as always I'm dying to finish
    the book I'm reading;
as always nine comes at some delicious
passage—Harriet Tubman breaking out!
    Freedom! I charge, staying put.

I am not now what I will be when dependency
is outgrown—or will it outgrow me,
    the book I'm reading
yield to other authorities: money, duty?
Day dwindles to inertia, a closed door impeding
    even second-hand light.

I have plans, Harriet Tubman, for my escape:
flashlight, blanket, book. I feel the shape
    of the book I'm reading
against my thighs like Moses' tablets scraped
with words, transgressive words, feeding
    a justice disobedient and late.

Correspondence

Amid catalogues, fliers, offers, bills,
Amid supermarket circulars shouting their hams
    and toilet-bowl cleaners,
Amid pleas for worthy causes, the cheap printing, the garish
    graphics—
Lo, a letter in the mailbox! its surface scarred with handwriting
        (wrinkles on the attentive brow of conversation),
    its address in cipher and semaphore (O flags of disposition,
        urging thy masters forward, to destiny!)
Behold the stamp kissed, affixed not by machine!
Behold the scale human, a handbreadth, the postmark red, a death
    day, a feast day,
Behold the sender who posted it from trouble, sister
    whose baby will not begin.

> *She wrote how she'd noticed that words and numbers*
> *Correspond—like "Lo," which is one and zero.*
> *There you have the sum of computer language:*
> *Infinite digits.*

> *"I don't usually fall for an interjection,*
> *But I'm fond of Lo, how it follows from its*
> *Form and function (calling attention to a*
> *Moment of wonder)."*

Webster's *dates it back to the Middle Ages.*
OED *denotes it a slimmed-down version*
Of "hello"—"Victorian thrift! Why waste time
Greeting each other?"

Here is the Lo of '01, my baby, the last letter I wrote:
He is a roly O lolling at the edge of vision, playing hard
to keep up with growth:
The ball moving at his push and pat,
The ball moving in kinetic conspiracy with itself,
The baby lifting against its droop his Capital O, his huge head
a peony bud on inadequate stem,
His eyes widened to O's,
His mouth wobbling to a wobbly O,
His expression concentrated, open but encircled,
the anticipation of amazement
while fixing upon judgment,
His discovery of roundness as friction defied and improved
upon,
His discovery of will as means to motion—
Such is the blossom of Lo, which resists its own sumptuous glut.

"Say the word out loud: you will make a joyful
noise. It cannot fail to be said with beauty.
Sound gives Lo the heft of enchantment, bird on
bough'd mathematics."

Words crowd upon me, rhymes and sorrows, by tens and multiples
    of ten, sesquipedalian—
Moments of wonder, jeweled and enameled, which cannot fail
    but might not become,
They crowd upon me, the mechanical offspring of gold.

The letter fairly flutters out of my hand, so fast is its flight
    from what truly matters,
So delicately has it not lit, a sappho, a hummingbird, upon its
                          subject.
I unfold mothpaper wings, reading her hand, reading
    what she does not write:
She does not write, *I am hollow, surrounded by foul omens.*
She does not write of the man and the woman seeking alchemy,
    their hearts in their mouths attending,
Their lovemaking tentative, the thermometers and egg timers
                         attending,
    the petri dish attending, somewhere too near, and syringes,
The man unable to penetrate, wilted,
She sighing, dry and unlovely,
Her O's low and sad, not the Lo! of ecstasy but of its opposite,
    enervation,
The lovely vowels of dolor, the lullaby of fallow, the gorgeous gong
    of moan,
He joins her long O, her river of O, confluent,
They pour their separate despairs through the O's of their eyes,
    the long, low barren O's of their mourning mouths.

It is utterly possible to grieve without loss. We call it desire.

> *"Don't forget, the angel announces with a*
> *Lo! the Christchild's birth. Why, the Bible's rife with*
> *Lo's, whenever someone delivers news of*
> *Ponderous import."*

> *"'You will get with child at the age of sixty.'*
> *'You will slay your son on an altar.' 'You, a*
> *Virgin, will conceive of an Agony both*
> *Blissful and Woeful.'"*

The unexpected arrives, the heralded comes not.
Lo! the rare babies, the ones addicted, defected, premature,
Lo! the three-year-old veteran of surgery,
Lo! the miscarriage after celebration and joy:
> It was the morning of the day of the shower,
> The crepe paper was strung on chandelier and candelabra,
> The table set with confetti and bright napkins, lo!
> The places laid, the guests each named in place—Suzy, Missy,
> Tammi, Lynette—
> Lo, she awoke to wet sheets, she awoke to bloody sheets,
> She rose and shed her celebration,
> The guests arrived to a note pinned to the curtain:
> > There has been a terrible mistake—

Lo, the orphan, the offspring of war or neglect,
Lo, the unfound birth mother, the child whose womb is abstract,
Lo, the envelop stamped with a hated old lover, a rapist, a Friend
of the Family,
the mother unable to bear the sight of him,
Lo, the child of a child, by her father.
And the common ones, in unremark'd abundance, the perfect ones,
The smallness of health and the newness of health,
The symmetry, digits in ten, and features in pairs,
The varieties of wail and squeal, the sameness of gesture
and universal accumulation of speech,
Lo unto them also.

And to the cluster of onlookers at the bank teller's line:
The townsfolk releasing their status as strangers,
The ages of other babies announced, and commented upon,
Their wont in matters of foodstuff and sleep,
Lo! this one's granddaughter speaks twelve words,
Lo! that one's great-niece speaks thirteen!
The confluence of lore, the pooling of data, the competitive eddies
of parents,
The entitlement of babies, and their unfailing demand,
Lo! the newborn that ever cometh, and another, lo!

These definitions have I carried on my hip,
Even as my correspondent carries their sore lack:
The burnished edges of bliss, of woe, calculated in hours,
The utter normalcy, which proves me lucky,

The fingers tenfold, a decade of toes.
The mobile revolves its gilded angels, peripheral, soulful—
Beautifully said, sad, each one raising a Lo,
proclaiming of wonder.

Mary at the Well

To be spared is no mercy. Each tug at the breast
lets down grief and life, indistinguishable rivulets.
The pale milk conjures maggoty ghosts while the sac
empties like Bethlehem after the governors execute
their office. A town devoid of children, a town
of stricken mothers, a town of empty wombs.
The mothers are quiet, so quiet in their grief.
The cribs are dumb. It is a kind of peace.

At the town well, the women lower their heads
at the sight of the unbearable Child, bouncing
and cooing in conspicuous health. For a time
before His coming they had forgotten, although
they never forget. How an infant's tiny heft pressures
hip, how sleep weighs, how suckles soften the babe.
For a moment each woman has her own child
back, bouncing and cooing, here at the town well.

Empty vessels go down into the well and return full.
No one is spared, not even Mary, who nurses
the dead alongside her Living One, who ponders
the holy stars, the generation of child-bodies.
(Where are they buried? How burnt? How cold?)
The well replenishes, full as a mass grave.

Details of Cana

That the water was transformed, yes, a miracle, but
that the resultant wine was good—ah, conviction,
sensing the presence of divinity in the guest
who exclaims to the host *but you've saved the best*
for last!—to smell a god in the mother asking her son
please, do something or the party will be ruined, ruined!

Cottonwood Tree, Woodbury County

for Marguerite McGuirk, on her 92nd birthday

She's old now, slack with Alzheimer's, but she once
stood clear-eyed where a creek sometimes ran, resisting
drought, her gnarled knuckles grazing hips,
her face not terribly plain, not terribly handsome.

All cottonwoods are always old forever,
despite the landscape she painted in her basement,
humming—that torn smock!—and squeezing ropes
of burnt sienna onto the bark-rough canvas.

She had white hair, a punishing decency.
You'd think that trick of shedding excess fluff
would generate distrust, but no, till lately
her linty drifts gave off an excess of comfort.

So she'd cook up Sloppy Joes in a dented
skillet, flour-sack hot pad for missing handle,
looking out the window at mussed grass, thinking
of red—those spiky canna, hot as onions!

thinking of brown, clumpy as ground beef.
Always dusting orphans with that wash-worn

white hair, sheets upstairs barely bespeaking
stripes. Their colors ran out late one year,

a time that wore no lipstick, whose tan freckles,
broadcast on tan cheeks, blurred the lines of features.
That's Marguerite, I'd say, a pioneer,
steadfast. That's white of her, the root of her.

A Mother's Favor Will Break Your Heart

Which is to walk home from school arriving just in time to hear
    the final cadenza of the Singer;
Which flourish accomplishes the end of her basting;
Which basting unlooses new apparel, new appall;

Which was sewn by hand, by her hand, by her
    hand come all the way from Butterick
    pattern picked for its pleating taste,
Which moved her to fabric store, bolts negotiated in their
                             cacophonous
    cubbyholes, plaids hollering, florals whimpering,
Which rendered pieces cut on the kitchen floor where the light
    reveals their volume;

Which are now orchestrated into yon smock-top matched-pant
    ensemble;
Which you must now try on, inside out, pins like tiny batons;
Which pansy collar descants upon painstaking interface;

Which is no time for craftsmanship;

Which is a fright and a heartbreak and a clutch of tenderest
    knives, this attempt, this kindness;

Which is to say your classmates who make fun of your clothes
      are nothing next to this:
Which is the wasted awful love that wrought you.

On the Feast of St. Margaret of Cortona

Saint Margaret, but to me, *Mamá.* And to the good
townspeople of Montepulciano, *La Putana,*
I remember them, *she gives it away, the whore.*

And Papá, I remember him, and our dog, leaping
through sticks and leaves to find him dead, and the grave
they threw together, and Papá's stiff eyelids, flimsy arms

flung out in an embrace that warmed to no one: gone
to happiness without us, as good as if he'd left
for yet another Other Woman. Now look at you, Mamá,

a saint! And look at me, your bastard, in my friar's robe,
still shivering, still thin as on the day Papá departed
and your hunt for something—agony? ecstasy?—began.

First you gave up everything we had: long cloaks,
crockery, domestics, gloves, our dog, the deep sigh
of thick silk tassels on your bedspread, familiarities and oils,

the pantry with its rows of spices stocked to bursting; oh,
the bread, baked every day as if it would never cease
to feed us, rising and regular, like breathing, like the sun . . .

The First Book of Kings puts Elisha to "plowing with twelve
yoke of oxen before him," when, suddenly, down comes a mantle
upon him. Elijah has called him, the good son, the plowman.
Elisha, who hesitates, says, "Let me kiss them, my father
and mother, and then will I follow thee." "Go back again," says
Elijah, dismantling the plowman, "for what have I done to thee?"

But in the Gospel according to Luke, when the Lord calls,
there is no such allowance for farewell returnings. "Lord, suffer
me first to go bury my father," says one who while unnamed,
is ever on record for failing Divine opportunity.
"Let the dead bury their dead," comes the Shepherd's reply.

Well, you were twenty-one, younger than I am now,
an easy age to walk away, Mamá, but always for you
it was easy to walk away. And so you left, we left,

first Montepulciano, then your father's house—
he'd have none of you anyway—and onward to the town
where purgatory began: Cortona, Cortona, Cortona.

We starved, Mamá, or *I* starved while you fasted,
enraptured, converted. And when food came
our way, despite your best intentions to elude it,

from Dona Raneria, or the Franciscans (were they
a bit alarmed at your intensity?) you gave it all away,
but not to me. I dined on piety. Remember how you fed

that loaf of bread—our first meal in three days!—
to the hag next door, dying in her filthy wools?
I was eight, Mamá, so hungry and no saint, no saint

at all, but I was beginning to learn the point of not
returning, like a great love not returned:
our best hope is the fire we swallow for ourselves.

> *Another, who like our Elisha wants only to bid*
> *a farewell, He will baptize "unfit" for God's kingdom, for once*
> *putting hand to the plough, one must never look back at one's parents.*

> *Meanwhile, Elisha, dismantled, unsure, reinterprets*
> *Elijah's ambiguous shrug: returns are verboten.*
> *So changing his tactics, he seizes on livestock, fillets one to feast*
> *his relations, which meets with Elijah's approval. But think*
> *of his family, losing their son to a prophecy, wouldn't*
> *that grief be enough without losing an ox? Our Elisha*
> *has rendered them doubly bereft, left the harvest imperiled*
> *for one final meal. O extravagant symbol, expensive as oxen!*

Mamá, your hairshirt was so coarse I bled to hug you.
That straw you'd break into shrapnel, weaving it through
your burlap skirt to make it hurt more—I ate that

straw, the closest I could come to your body's warmth,
persisting. Now I understood: your warmth persisted,
nothing you could do would ever stamp it out.

It melted straw, it softened burlap, it plumped your lips,
your breasts, your hips, which hunger made more beautiful,
while I turned scabby with every favor you refused.

> *Later, in Kings, a diastole. After a great wind,*
> *a mighty wild wind "rent the mountains, and brake into pieces*
> *the rocks," after earthquake, that mocking of mother-rocked cradles,*
> *and soon after fire, "a still small voice" comes forth:*
> *A child's voice, God, whom only prophets hear.*

When I spoke, my gods did not hear. Today, your day,
I display myself, a relic like the bits of bone and hair
that traumatize the altar. At nightfall, I will feast.

Salutations

Let jubilant cries issue forth, the rivers rise in animistic steam,
For thou art holy and whole, ordeal and pact.
For thou sittest at the right hand of Praise and Affection.
For thy throated flute, pipe and reed are as a charm
       of goldfinches
    revolving in brilliant sound and light.
For thy sorrow is as windlestraws blown forth and curling.
Sleep drifts about thee in dunes.

Within thee anvil, hammer and stirrup, Sir Wimble-finger,
       Gimlet-Eye,
    Lord of Chuck and Whistle,
All tools of thy creation are contained within thee,
    the pretty mechanics arranged and ready within thee,
    the microscopic codices scrolled, precise as drill bits
       within thee,
    the coda, thy mortality, also within thee.
For thou art inconceivable, conceived in a leap: act
       and imagination
    fused, the one partaking fully of the other,
    simultaneous but separate.
For thou art even as pain, both source and message:
    pinprick and its scattering of needles (so playful
       in their jangled dance of silver),

distant star and lightshed, spread across
      the firmament of thy skull, Master Wishbone,
Master Squirm-o'-the-Bunting, Master Grace.

And now thou belchest constellations, vaporous
      and alive with humors,
They encircle thee, swirling about in rapturous tendrils,
      Baron Finch, Prince Windlestraw,
For thou art light, its emission, and that which it falleth upon,
Claims outrageous, gastronomical.

For thou art landscape entire, Umbilicus Most Potent,
A planet, a globe, encompassing all.
It hangs within thee annealing (now art thou tempered)
      tucked, rounded, curled as thou art,
Universal,
One poem.

Notes

Dedication is from *Marco Polo Sings a Solo*, by John Guare.

"Brown-Headed Cowbirds," p. 24

The text for the epigraphs is quoted directly from *The Audubon Society Field Guide to North American Birds, Eastern Region*. John Bull and John Farrand, Jr., Knopf, New York. © 1977. (p. 559)

"It Was a Normal Day Except I Fell," p. 32

The poem ends on an echo of a line from Sylvia Plath's "Nick and the Candlestick": "O love, how did you get here?"

"Ivory-Billed Woodpecker," p. 35

I am indebted to Jonathan Rosen's article "The Ghost Bird," in *The New Yorker* of May 14, 2001, for his description of the logging incident of 1938, for the epigraph to section VI, and for his excellent characterization of the ivorybill upon which I have relied throughout.

The source for the epigraphs of all other sections is Richard H. Pough's *Audubon Bird Guide: Small Land Birds of Eastern & Central North America from Southern Texas to Central Greenland*. Doubleday & Co., New York. © 1946. (pp. 50–51)

For what scant details exist about George Stinney's sentencing and execution I have relied on several Web sites, among them soundportraits.org and crimelibrary.com.

"The Visual Display of Quantitative Information," p. 55
The title is taken from a book by Edward R. Tufte, *The Visual Display of Quantitative Information*, © 1983, Graphics Press, Connecticut.

"Mercy School," p. 64
The sources for the epigraphs are as follows:

Essay One: from the chapter "Unquestioned Trust," p. 194, *The Marriage Spirit: Finding the Passion and Joy of Soul-Centered Love*, by Drs. Evelyn and Paul Moschetta. Simon & Schuster, New York, © 1998 by Paul Moschetta and Evelyn Moschetta.

Essay Two: from the chapter "Being Here Now," p. 38, *Handbook to Higher Consciousness*, by Ken Keyes, Jr. Third Edition. Living Love Center, Berkely, California, © 1973.

Essay Three: The first epigraph is from chapter 4, "Start by Building Self-Esteem," p. 64, of *Feeling Good: The New Mood Therapy*, by David D. Burns, M.D. Quill/HarperCollins, 2000. © 1980 by David Burns. The second epigraph is from the chapter "Goodness: The Miracle of Change," p. 234, *The Marriage Spirit: Finding the Passion and Joy of Soul-Centered Love*, by Drs. Evelyn and Paul Moschetta. Simon & Schuster, New York. © 1998 by Paul Moschetta and Evelyn Moschetta.

Essay Four: from the chapter "The Two Joyous Centers," p. 75, *Handbook to Higher Consciousness*, by Ken Keyes, Jr. Third Edition. Living Love Center, Berkeley, California, © 1973.

"Stray," p. 73

"Hot salt" is again from Sylvia Plath. In her poem "Medusa" she writes "I am sick to death of hot salt."

"Loose Leaf from a Destroyed Journal," p. 79

The epigraph is from the introduction to Sylvia Plath's *Collected Poems*, © 1981 by Ted Hughes. Page 13, HarperPerennial ed., New York.

"Coney Island," p. 84

John McKane was a Brooklyn-based nineteenth-century real estate developer and Tammany Hall crony whose control over Coney Island was equal parts absolute and lawless.

"Rural Development News," p. 99

The quotations are from an article as cited in vol. 23 no. 3, 1999, of *Rural Development News*, a newsletter published by the Agriculture Department of Iowa State University.